Tranquility
The Piano Solos of Phil Coulter

In the whole 'Tranquility' concept, the real stars are the
melodies. Some are songs, hundreds of years old, which I have known
since childhood. Others are my own compositions which are important
to me, for a variety of reasons. I love each one of these tunes
and I get continuing pleasure from playing them.

This book comes in answer to thousands of requests for the
printed music of my recorded arrangements. You don't have to be
a virtuoso pianist by any means to play these special transcriptions.
Indeed, some of them will be easy, even for children.
My hope is that this volume will give other pianists, young
or old, beginner or veteran, a share in the many hours of happiness
I have derived from playing this music.

Wishing you Peace and Tranquility,

Phil Coulter

Phil Coulter

Exclusive distributors:
Hal Leonard
7777 West Bluemound Road, Milwaukee, WI 53213
Email: info@halleonard.com
Hal Leonard Europe Limited
42 Wigmore Street Maryleborne, London, WIU 2 RN
Email: info@halleonardeurope.com
Hal Leonard Australia Pty. Ltd.
4 Lentara Court Cheltenham, Victoria, 9132 Australia
Email: info@halleonard.com.au

This book © Copyright 1986 by
Hal Leonard
ISBN 0.7119.0944.X
Order No. AM 63280
Art direction by Mike Bell
Designed by Tracey Cunnell
Arranged by Frank Booth and Phil Coulter
All songs selected and edited by Phil Coulter

Printed in EU.

www.halleonard.com

THE DERRY AIR

(Traditional) Arranged by Phil Coulter.

One of the most famous of all Irish melodies, it was first collected as a fiddle tune at Limavady, Co. Derry.
Much later, words were added and it became an international favourite as 'Danny Boy.'
This arrangement has a touch of "country" piano.

THE SPINNING WHEEL

By J F Waller. Arranged by Phil Coulter.

How well I remember this song, on an old 78 record, sung by the wonderful Delia Murphy.
This is the most requested of all the songs I've recorded.

9

CARRICKFERGUS

(Traditional) Arranged by Phil Coulter.

The Irish are great travellers, but love to savour the bitter-sweet taste of homesickness.
Some of our best songs have been born out of the sadness of separation. This one is a classic.

14

15

MAGGIE

By J A Butterfield. Arranged by Phil Coulter.

There are as many versions of this song as there are theories about its origin. Some say it comes from Ireland, others that it was written in Canada. No matter, it must be one of the most recognized tunes in the world.

17

MY LAGAN LOVE

(Traditional) Arranged by Phil Coulter.

Undoubtedly, one of the loveliest and most characteristically Irish of all her folk tunes. The plaintive melody and modal harmonies give a wonderful haunting quality. My advice is to learn this one until you can close your eyes and play from your heart!

STEAL AWAY

By Phil Coulter.

I wrote and recorded this wee song first with my old friends The Furey Brothers.
We always play it in our concert programme and audiences love to join in and sing along.

23

MARY FROM DUNGLOE

(Traditional) Arranged by Phil Coulter.

Donegal is sort of my spiritual home and this is one of the finest Donegal songs I know,
from a little village that is every bit as lovely as the melody.

tacet ‑ ‑ ‑ * A

Left Hand

(Melody)

Right Hand

26

27

28

LOVE THEE DEAREST

By Thomas Moore. Arranged by Phil Coulter.

A kind of Irish parlour song, this is a real favourite with Irish tenors and has probably been murdered more than most other tunes. As with many other songs, I have tried to strip all those associations away and let the melody speak for itself, in a simple uncomplicated arrangement.

BUACHAILL O'N EIRNE

(Traditional) Arranged by Phil Coulter.

As a child I learned this beautiful song in the Gaeltacht in West Donegal, and it has stayed with me through the years. It is sometimes sung, in a slightly adapted version, as 'Come By The Hills.'

34

LOVE'S OLD SWEET SONG

By J L Molloy. Arranged by Phil Coulter.

Also known as 'Just a Song at Twilight,' the opening line of the chorus.
The changeover from 4/4 in the verse to 3/4 in the chorus is most attractive.
I really love to play this tune.

THE TOWN I LOVED SO WELL

By Phil Coulter.

A song about my home town, Derry, this has become a sort of anthem in Ireland. There is so much
I could say about the song, but suffice to say that it has given me more satisfaction
than any other song I've ever written. Be gentle with this one.

Flowingly with nostalgia (♩ = 100)

BOULAVOGUE
(Traditional) Arranged by Phil Coulter.

A strong song from Co. Wexford about a famous incident during the 1798 rebellion. This was one of the most bloody events in Irish history and the tune evokes all the pain and the passion of the battlefield.

41

42

LAKE OF SHADOWS

By Phil Coulter.

I have a house in Buncrana, Co. Donegal, on the shores of Lough Swilly, a stretch of water which
is sometimes breathtaking in its beauty, sometimes chilling in its unpredictable savagery.
It is known locally as The Lake Of Shadows.

44

45

TRANQUILITY
By Phil Coulter.

I called this tune 'Tranquility' because I couldn't think of anything else to call it!
It has quite a simple melody, over a pulsing rhythm, with a feel that is
probably more contemporary than many of the other tunes.

47

THE LAST ROSE OF SUMMER

By Thomas Moore. Arranged by Phil Coulter.

A fine example of the Anglo-Irish school of music and lyrics, written by the prolific Thomas Moore.
This lovely song was said to be a particular favourite of the first Irish superstar,
Count John McCormack! It has a very simple accompaniment but treat it with respect.

50

A BUNCH OF THYME

(Traditional) Arranged by Phil Coulter.

A very popular song in Ireland. Loved probably more for its simple catchiness than for any great beauty.
Once again, in this arrangement, the piano has a slight 'country' feel.

THE GREEN GLENS OF ANTRIM

(Traditional) Arranged by Phil Coulter.

The best emigrant songs, and this is certainly one, have very evocative melodies
and very emotional lyrics. This one is inspired by a particularly beautiful
place with a very strong sense of Irish music and tradition.

56

THE FLIGHT OF THE EARLS
By Phil Coulter.

In the early 1600's a group of Irish noblemen sailed out of Rathmullan on the shores of Lough Swilly. They were part of a general exodus, fleeing before advancing English armies, seeking refuge in the courts of France and Spain. The continuing part played in Irish history by those European countries fascinates me, and I wrote this piece to evoke the period.

59

60

THE CLIFFS OF DOONEEN

(Traditional) Arranged by Phil Coulter.

I first heard this tune sung many years ago by Christy Moore, when I was producing the superb Planxty.
This is a very easy arrangement of a beautiful simple melody.